CRUCIFIXION of Poverty

DR. D. K. OLUKOYA

CRUCIFIXION OF POVERTY

© 2013 DR. D. K. OLUKOYA

ISBN: 978-978-920-057-3

Published - May, 2013

Published by:
The Battle Cry Christian Ministries
322, Herbert Macaulay Street, Sabo, Yaba
P. O. Box 12272, Ikeja, Lagos.
www.battlecrystore.com
email: info@battlecrystore.com
customercare@battlecrystore.com
sales@battlecrystore.com
Phone: 0803-304-4239, 01-8044415.

I salute my wonderful wife, Pastor Shade, for her invaluable support in the ministry.
I appreciate her unquantifiable support in the book ministry as the cover designer, art editor and art adviser.

All the Scriptures are from the King James Version

All rights reserved. Reproduction in whole or part without a written permission is prohibited. Printed in Nigeria.

CONTENTS

CHAPTER	PAGE
1. Crucifixion Of Poverty	4-12
2. Breaking The Bounds Of Affliciton And Poverty	13-31
3. My Story Must Change To Glory	32-45

CHAPTER One

CRUCIFIXION of Poverty

You must read and digest this scripture because this is not the kind of message you get often.

> *Jesus said: "the Spirit of the Lord is upon Me, because He has anointed me to preach the gospel to the poor, heal the broken hearted, preach deliverance to the captives, recovery of sight to the blind, to set at liberty them that are bruised, and preach the acceptable year of the Lord"* Luke 4:18-19.

The first thing that anointing did was to break the backbone of poverty. When He said 'the poor' he means the poor in all ramifications: spiritually poor, physically poor, maritally poor, materially poor, financially poor, mentally poor, etc.

> *'For you know the grace of our Lord Jesus Christ, for though He was rich, yet for your sakes, He became poor, that you*

> *through His poverty may be rich.'*
> 2 Corinthians 8:9.

When you talk about finances, you are talking about MONEY.

WHAT IS MONEY?

MONEY is the most acceptable form of exchange. It is controlled by a spirit called mammon. Until we know how to deal with it, we cannot enjoy true riches. Money has a caging influence, it has turned itself to the greatest idol. Majority of people in this world have been captured by the school of money worshippers.

Many have gone to places they should not have gone because of money. Many have eaten and swallowed what they should not really have eaten or swallowed because of money. Many have been suffering in strange lands because of money. Money is a deceiver and could give you sicknesses that nobody can cure.

Money has deceived many girls into breaking their virginity in shame and selling their bodies.

Money has made many people to suck human blood, it has even changed the vision of so many great men of God today. As you are reading this book, I have a long list of so-called men of God that money has destroyed their calling. Money has also destroyed many destinies. It can be put you in direct confrontation with your destiny.

That is why a man could kill his own wife or his own mother for ritual in order to be rich. No wonder the Bible says, "It is the blessing of the Lord that maketh rich and added no sorrow to it". Quick money is quick death, but when you are hard-working, and you are patient, God will bless you and you will not gather the wealth of sorrow.

Money has a voice and to listen to its voice is to marry a cobra. It is an ancient power, and it's strong and deceitful. It controls fools and makes them to do all kinds of evil things.

Most times if you find people fighting in a church, and the church splits into two or three, you can be sure that it is not far-fetched from money.

FINANCIAL DELIVERANCE

The first deliverance many people need is the deliverance from the grip of the spirit of mammon. Financial deliverance means seven things:

1. Freedom from debt.
2. Eating what you want and not just what you see.
3. Not being dependent on your parents or others for your livelihood or sustenance.
4. Adequate provision for yourself and your family.
5. Having basic needs of life (food, shelter clothing and health) met.
6. Having more income than expenditure.
7. Being able to lend and not borrow.

WHY WE NEED FINANCIAL DELIVERANCE?

1. To have a full and a fulfilled life.
2. To manifest the glory of God.
3. To appropriate your redemption rights.
4. The destinies of many people are attached to ours, and we need to carry their burden.
5. To be able to further the things of God's kingdom.
6. Because poverty is demonic and is a killer. Do you know that millions of people die of malaria every year just because of poverty? If poverty is removed, malaria will stop killing people. Somebody is supposed to buy insecticide but cannot afford it because of poverty.
7. To lay up treasures for ourselves in heaven.

If you will pray with holy violence and holy anger, the chain of debt the enemy has tied around your neck will be broken. You need to aggressively demand your financial freedom because if you are not financially free, you are not free indeed, no matter how big your idea is. You cannot succeed without money, and if you allow the devil to steal your money, he can paralyse your life. If you don't tie down what God has given you, the enemy will take it away.

It is a tragedy when you are supposed to be a mountain-mover but the hands with which to move the mountain have been cut-off by poverty. There was a woman I met in U.S.A. If she were standing here now and someone is broke and wants to know who to go to beg for money, with the way she looks and carries herself, she would be the one one will go to. But she doesn't have one cent. Anywhere she goes, they believe she is very rich; in fact people go to her to borrow money but they are now surprised when she says, "I have not eaten breakfast." The anointing for wealth is upon her but the enemy has buried it. Can you close your eyes and shout this prayer loud and clear:

Every power, delegated to bury my wealth, you are a liar, DIE! in the name of Jesus.

PRAYER POINTS

1. My wealth, buried in the earth, come forth, in the name of Jesus.
2. Every arrow of witchcraft fired into my prosperity, DIE, in the name of Jesus.
3. Garments of poverty, CATCH FIRE, in the name of Jesus.
4. You financial killer of my father's house, I am not your candidate, therefore, DIE, in the name of Jesus.
5. You financial killer of my mother's house, I am not your candidate, therefore, DIE, in the name of Jesus.
6. Expected and unexpected financial breakthroughs, LOCATE ME BY FIRE, in the name of Jesus.
7. Poverty activator dream, hear the WORD of the Lord, S-C-A-T-T-E-R, in the name of Jesus.
8. Every virtue of my life, buried by household wickedness, come out by fire, in the name of Jesus.

9. O heavens over my prosperity, OPEN BY FIRE, in the name of Jesus.
10. O wealth, JUMP OUT of the habitation of the wicked, and LOCATE ME NOW, in the name of Jesus.
11. Angels of the living God, PURSUE WEALTH INTO MY HANDS, in the name of Jesus.
12. I ATTACK my lack with the SWORD OF FIRE, in the name of Jesus.
13. I REMOVE my name from the book of financial embarrassment, in the name of Jesus.
14. I BIND the spirit of DEBT; I SHALL NOT BORROW TO EAT, in the name of Jesus.
15. I retrieve my purse from the hand of Judas, in the name of Jesus.
16. Let divine magnet of prosperity, be planted in my hands, in the name of Jesus.
17. I BIND every word spoken against my breakthroughs, in the name of Jesus.
18. I TAKE OVER the WEALTH of the gentiles, in the name of Jesus.
19. Lord Jesus, as from today, hold my purse, in the name of Jesus.

▶ CHAPTER

Breaking
the BOUNDS
of AFFLICTION
and
POVERTY

CRUCIFIXION OF POVERTY

Oh that men would praise the LORD for his goodness, and for his wonderful works to the children of men! 9 For he satisfieth the longing soul, and filleth the hungry soul with goodness. 10 Such as sit in darkness and in the shadow of death, being bound in affliction and iron; 11 Because they rebelled against the words of God, and contemned the counsel of the most High: 12 Therefore he brought down their heart with labour; they fell down, and there was none to help. 13 Then they cried unto the LORD in their trouble, and he saved them out of their distresses. 14 He brought them out of darkness and the shadow of death, and brake their bands in sunder. Psalm 107:8-14.

What is affliction?

Affliction is a condition of suffering, pain, distress, and calamity, imposed by illness, loss or misfortune. It is anything causing pain, suffering and distress. It is an entity, a spirit. It can be regarded as a trial, the trial that tries people's endurance. It can be regarded as tribulation and misfortune that applies to a circumstance or event. There are cries of the afflicted in the Bible:

Many personalities in the Bible were afflicted and came out gloriously. We have personalities such as Hannah, Job, David, Ruth and so on. Hannah cried to the Lord in her condition which she called an affliction. Here Hannah calls bareness, affliction.

> *And she vowed a vow, and said, O LORD of hosts, if thou wilt indeed look on the affliction of thine handmaid, and remember me, and not forget thine handmaid, but wilt give unto thine handmaid a man child,*

> *then I will give him unto the LORD all the days of his life, and there shall no razor come upon his head.* I Sam 1:11.

David cried in Psalm 25:16 Turn thee unto me, and have mercy upon me; for I am desolate and afflicted.

Also hear his cry again in Psalm 94:16-18:

> *Who will rise up for me against the evildoers? or who will stand up for me against the workers of iniquity? Unless the LORD had been my help, my soul had almost dwelt in silence. When I said, My foot slippeth; thy mercy, O LORD, held me up.*

David cried against the evil doers and the workers of iniquity who assigned evils against his soul. Jonah lamented in Jonah 2:2:, I cried by reason of mine affliction unto the LORD, and he heard me; out of the belly of hell cried I, and thou heardest my voice.

Jonah went through a condition of life and death. He called that an affliction. His predicament came as a result of disobedient. Therefore, number one reason that affliction will come upon a person is disobedience. Affliction has a day and time of manifestation. By this I mean, it has the day and time when it comes upon man. Job knew this spiritual reality when he lamented in Job 30:16: *And now my soul is poured out upon me; the days of affliction have taken hold upon me.*

> *My bones are pierced in me in the night season: and my sinews take no rest.* Job 30:17.

> *The LORD said, Verily it shall be well with thy remnant; verily I will cause the enemy to entreat*

> *thee well in the time of evil and in the time of affliction.* Jer 15:11.

> *O LORD, my strength, and my fortress, and my refuge in the day of affliction, the Gentiles shall come unto thee from the ends of the earth, and shall say, Surely our fathers have inherited lies, vanity, and things wherein there is no profit.* Jeremiah 16:19.

THE POWER OF AFFLICTION

Affliction has cords with which it ties people down.

> *And if they be bound in fetters, and be holden in cords of affliction;* Job 36:8.

The Bible clearly says that a person can be held down by the cords of affliction. When someone is cast down or loses a battle, whether spiritual or physical' and refuses to rise up to confront the failure, such a person is being held down by the cords of affliction.

There is bread and water of affliction:

> *And say, Thus saith the king, Put this fellow in the prison, and feed him with bread of affliction and with water of affliction, until I return in peace.* II Chronicles 18:26
> *And though the Lord give you the bread of adversity, and the water of affliction, yet shall not thy teachers be removed into a corner any more, but thine eyes shall see thy teachers* Isaiah 30:20.

Human agents can feed a person with the bread and water of affliction. When someone looks at you and says he hates you for no reason, to the point of firing you from your job, he is trying to feed you with bread and water of affliction of sorrow. Just as king Ahab purposed to keep Prophet Micaiah in prison to eat and drink in agony for daring to prophesy by God, so also evil men try to make people eat and drink in sorrow. Men also can be fed with the bread and water of affliction by God, when they choose to live in sin and disobedience.

Affliction is bitter. All afflictions are bitter. But satan and his hosts try hard to make an affliction very bitter. By the time the adversary and his hosts have got the condition of an individual to a very bitter level, only a persistent cry onto the Lord can save the individual from complete destruction.

> *For the LORD saw the affliction of Israel, that it was very bitter: for there was not any shut up, nor any left, nor any helper for Israel.*
> II Kings 14:26.

Affliction binds:

> *Such as sit in darkness and in the shadow of death, being bound in affliction and iron;* Psalms 107:10.

Job was bound in the affliction of disease and sorrow resulting from the loss of his children and all his belongings, until God intervened. Hannah was bound in the affliction of barrenness, until she cried to the Lord and the Lord intervened.

The bounds of affliction must be broken in the name of Jesus.

Affliction brings low:

> *Again, they are minished and brought low through oppression, affliction, and sorrow.*
> Psalms 107:39.

The affliction that came against the life of Job brought him down from a highly exalted position to a position of irrelevance and dishonor. At one time Job said that young children despised and spoke against him – Job 19:18.

Affliction brings into captivity:

> *Judah is gone into captivity because of affliction, and because of great servitude: she dwelleth among the heathen, she findeth no rest: all her persecutors overtook her between the straits.* Lamentation 1:3.

Affliction can be projected and assigned. The predicaments that befell Job are good examples of how satan can assign and project affliction against a person.

Who are the other projectors and assigners of affliction?
1.   Demons and evil spirits.
2.   Ancestral spirits.
3.   Environmental spirits.

4. Envious friends.
5. Envious family members.
6. Witches and wizards.
7. Occult personalities.

WHAT ARE THE REASONS FOR AFFLICTION?

➢ *Your right standing before the Lord.* A person can be afflicted because he is standing right before the Lord. Job was a good example of this kind of unjust attack.

➢ *Your divine purpose or assignment in life.* God told Jeremiah from the beginning what shall befall him as he walks in obedience to Him. But Jeremiah forgot too soon when he later lamented

> *Shall evil be recompensed for good? for they have digged a pit for my soul. Remember that I stood before thee to speak good for them, and to turn away thy wrath from them.* Jeremiah 18:20.

CRUCIFIXION OF POVERTY

Your sins

> *Fools because of their transgression, and because of their iniquities, are afflicted.*
> Psalms 107:17.

> *Why criest thou for thine affliction? thy sorrow is incurable for the multitude of thine iniquity: because thy sins were increased, I have done these things unto thee.*
> Jeremiah 30:15.

How does God respond to affliction?
The face of the Lord is upon the affliction of the afflicted.

> *For he hath not despised nor abhorred the affliction of the afflicted; neither hath he hid his face from him; but when he cried unto him, he heard.* Psalms 22:24.

The Psalmist makes us realise that God did not turn away His face from the afflicted. The persistent cry of the afflicted always comes before the Lord. And He will surely respond and comfort.

God will save the afflicted:

> *For thou wilt save the afflicted people; but wilt bring down high looks. There are people who are under the siege of various afflictions.* Psalms 18:27.

The word of God says that. He will save the afflicted people. He will shield you from wicked afflictions currently bombarding you. He will protect you. All you need is to cry to Him and He will save you.

God delivers those who are in affliction:

> *He delivereth the poor in his affliction, and openeth their ears in oppression.* Job 36:15.

CRUCIFIXION OF POVERTY

Perhaps you have been held captive by the power of one affliction or the other, there is hope for you. For the word of God says that. He delivers the poor in his affliction. He is ready to deliver you, because the word of God is God Himself.
God's promise to the afflicted.

> *What do ye imagine against the LORD? he will make an utter end: affliction shall not rise up the second time.* Nah 1:9.

God has promised us in His word that He shall bring affliction to an immediate end. And that it shall never rise up again the second time. Amen.

HOW TO BREAK THE BOUNDS OF AFFLICTION

If you are living in sin, repent. Confess your sins unto the Lord.

Look upon mine affliction and my pain; and forgive all my sins. Obey the commandments of the Lord. Psalms 25:18.

Consider mine affliction, and deliver me: for I do not forget thy law. Psalms 119:153.

Use the word of God to break the bounds of affliction.

This is my comfort in my affliction: for thy word hath quickened me. Psalms 119:50.

CRY UNTO THE LORD

Nevertheless he regarded their affliction, when he heard their cry: Psalms 106:44.

> *Then Jonah prayed unto the LORD his God out of the fish's belly, And said, I cried by reason of mine affliction unto the LORD, and he heard me; out of the belly of hell cried I, and thou heardest my voice.* Jon 2:1-2.

Pray warfare prayers after the order of Jeremiah.

> *Then said they, Come, and let us devise devices against Jeremiah; for the law shall not perish from the priest, nor counsel from the wise, nor the word from the prophet. Come, and let us smite him with the tongue, and let us not give heed to any of his words. Give heed to me, O LORD, and hearken to the voice of them that contend with me. Shall evil be recompensed for good? for they have digged a pit for my soul. Remember that I stood before thee to speak good for them, and to*

turn away thy wrath from them. Therefore deliver up their children to the famine, and pour out their blood by the force of the sword; and let their wives be bereaved of their children, and be widows; and let their men be put to death; let their young men be slain by the sword in battle. Let a cry be heard from their houses, when thou shalt bring a troop suddenly upon them: for they have digged a pit to take me, and hid snares for my feet. Yet, LORD, thou knowest all their counsel against me to slay me: forgive not their iniquity, neither blot out their sin from thy sight, but let them be overthrown before thee; deal thus with them in the time of thine anger.
Jeremiah 18:18-23.

PRAYER POINTS

Prayers that break the bounds of afflictions are outlined below:

1. Begin your prayer by thanking Jesus for making provision for your deliverance by His blood that was shed on the cross of Calvary.
2. Confess all known sins in your life loud and clear to the Lord and ask for forgiveness.
3. God, visit me today and crush the power of affliction over my life, in the name of Jesus.
4. By the blood of Jesus, I overthrow the power of affliction that has made me irrelevant in my generation, in the name of Jesus.
5. I hold the rod of God in my hand and I break the bounds of affliction that is set to make me a nonentity in my generation, in the name of Jesus.

6. Thou God that delivered Job from his affliction, deliver me today from every affliction afflicting my destiny, in the name of Jesus.
7. Every power assigned to afflict my finances, perish, in the name of Jesus.
8. Every affliction binding me to failure, break by the power of God, in the name of Jesus.
9. Poverty affliction, die in my life, in the name of Jesus.
10. Disease and sickness affliction, die in my life, in the name of Jesus.
11. Marital-destroying affliction, die in my life, in the name of Jesus.
12. Loneliness affliction, die in my life, in the name of Jesus.
13. Glory of God, overshadow me now and break the bounds of affliction assigned over my life (my marriage, my health, my career), in the name of Jesus.
14. Father God, by Your name Jehovah, the man of war, arise and visit with instant deliverance, the affliction that has kept me below my divine position, in the name of Jesus.

CHAPTER Three

My STORY must CHANGE *to* GLORY

1. Good things closed against me, OPEN, in the name of Jesus.
2. Every yoke holding me, BREAK, in the name of Jesus.
3. MY story shall change to glory, in the name of Jesus.
4. My God will arise and permanently stop my tears, in the name of Jesus.
5. If I must cry, it shall be a cry of joy, in the name of Jesus.
6. Satanic blankets covering my glory, CATCH FIRE, in the name of Jesus.
7. Every power gathered to disgrace me, I scatter you into powder, in the name of Jesus.
8. I uproot obstacles to my testimonies, in the name of Jesus.
9. O God, arise and do what will make men to notice You in my life, in the name of Jesus.
10. Curse of seeing good things but not obtaining them, BREAK, in the name of Jesus.
11. My cup of breakthroughs, BEGIN TO RUN OVER, in the name of Jesus.
12. I shall not miss my divine allocation, in the name of Jesus.

CRUCIFIXION OF POVERTY

13. My divine provision, LOCATE ME, in the name of Jesus.
14. Every evil label assigned to my life, blood of Jesus, FLUSH THEM OUT, in the name of Jesus.
15. I shall obtain practical awesome results, in the name of Jesus.
16. I shall be for signs and wonders, in the name of Jesus.
17. I shall talk less and testify more, in the name of Jesus.
18. I shall taste the awesome power of God in every area of my life, in the name of Jesus.
19. This shall be my season of overcoming laughter, and victory dance, in the name of Jesus.
20. The God that made Abraham to testify, shall secure my celebration, in the name of Jesus.
21. The Lord that caused Daniel to be celebrated shall secure my celebration, in the name of Jesus.
22. The Lord that destroyed the garment of shame assigned to blind Bartimaeus, shall make shame a stranger to my life, in the name of Jesus.

23. I shall have overcoming victory laughter, in the name of Jesus.
24. My testimonies shall be awesome because it cannot be explained, in the name of Jesus.
25. This is my season of laughter by the power in the blood of Jesus.
26. By the power in the blood of Jesus, I will sing my song and dance my dance, in the name of Jesus.
27. I shall have more than enough, I shall not want, in the name of Jesus.
28. I declare that my season of uncommon breakthrough has come, in the name of Jesus.
29. My ways shall not be stagnant, in the name of Jesus.
30. I shall sing a new song and dance a new dance, in the name of Jesus.
31. Let every evil shadow be melted by Holy Ghost fire, in the name of Jesus.
32. I break and cancel with the blood of Jesus every evil mark, incision and writing, placed in my spirit and body as a result of my membership of evil associations and I purify my body, soul and spirit with Holy Ghost fire, in the name of Jesus.

33. I purge myself with the blood of Jesus of all evil food I have ever eaten in the evil world and I purify myself with the fire of the Holy Ghost, in the name of Jesus.
34. Lord, send Holy Ghost fire into my root and burn out all unclean things deposited in it by spirit husband and wife, in the name of Jesus.
35. Lord, let the Holy Ghost fire effect immediate breakthrough in every area of my life, in the name of Jesus.
36. Holy Ghost fire, incubate my life with your freshness and refreshing power, in the name of Jesus.
37. Holy Ghost, circulate all over my body, in the name of Jesus.
38. Holy Ghost, occupy every area vacated by the spirit of uncertainty in my mind, in the name of Jesus.
39. I receive the confronting anointing and power of the Holy Ghost, in the name of Jesus.
40. I receive the unsearchable wisdom in the Holy Ghost, in the name of Jesus.
41. Holy Ghost fire, purge my life completely, in the name of Jesus.

42. Holy Ghost fire, fall upon my eyes and burn to ashes every evil force and all satanic powers controlling my eyes, in the name of Jesus.
43. Holy Ghost fire, destroy every satanic garment in my life, in the name of Jesus.
44. Holy Ghost fire, grant me a glimpse of your glory now, in the name of Jesus.
45. Pour the Father's jealousy upon me now, in the name of Jesus.
46. Holy Ghost, quicken me, in the name of Jesus.
47. Holy Ghost, breath on me now, in the name of Jesus.
48. Holy Ghost, fill me that I may bring forth healing power, in the name of Jesus.
49. Let the blood of Jesus and the fire of the Holy Ghost cleanse every organ in my body, in the name of Jesus.
50. Father, let the fire of the Holy Ghost enter into my bloodstream and cleanse my system, in the name of Jesus.
51. Holy Ghost fire, destroy every garment of reproach in my life, in the name of Jesus.

CRUCIFIXION OF POVERTY

> *The LORD maketh poor, and maketh rich: he bringeth low, and lifteth up. He raiseth up the poor out of the dust, and lifteth up the beggar from the dunghill, to set them among princes, and to make them inherit the throne of glory: for the pillars of the earth are the LORD's, and he hath set the world upon them.* 1 Sam 2:7-8.

In the Bible passage above it is crystal clear that promotion belongs unto God. Under which canopy does the Lord raise the poor, the beggar and set them among the princes? The Bible gives us the answer

> *A good man obtaineth favour of the LORD: but a man of wicked devices will he condemn.*
> Prov 12:2.

Divine favour is what every man needs. There is no amount of limitation that divine favour cannot remove. Through divine favour many have won battles.

Through divine favour many have become heroes. Through divine favour many become kings. By divine favour confirmed failures have became successful. Through divine favour you can secure the willingness of God to bless and protect you.

THE OIL

If you need complete victory you need the oil of favour on your head. If you want satanic agents to be your footstool, you need the oil of favour upon your head. Even in the times of temptation and trials favour will sustain you. When others are falling and you are almost stumbling, divine favour will lift you up.

A servant who has won divine favour will be treated with honour and respect. A servant with divine favour will enjoy the privileges of freedom. When you have the oil of favour on your head, it becomes so easy for you to have breakthroughs. The oil of favour upon your head will uplift you. The oil of favour will remove the obstacles on your way and make you a celebrity.

OASIS IN YOUR DESERT

With the oil of favour on your head even a desert situation will become the garden of Eden. The oil of favour will change your mountain to a plain ground. The oil of favour will turn your impossibilities to possibilities. When you have the oil of favour on your head you have the concentration of God's presence that can do all things for you. You will achieve spectacular feats in times of challenges.

Without the oil of favour, tragedy can occur and wipe you out. When divine favour is in your life, you will command respect. When divine favour is upon your head, all your enemy's efforts will be futile.

Divine favour can make you a mystery to those who are around you. Divine favour can make you to be like a lamb among wolves and they cannot come near you. Divine favour will make you to become a spectacle that the angels of the Lord will be watching with interest.

DIVINE FAVOUR

Divine favour will make you a wonder to your contemporaries. It will counter the spirit of Balaam that comes against you. With divine favour upon you God answers every prayer you say.

Divine favour will draw red marks upon you so that you cannot be touched by your enemy. Divine favour will give you the key to uncommon promotion. If you want to be highly lifted you must have the oil of favour on your head.

There are different kinds of oils. There are negative and positive oils. When the oil of divine favour is upon you, people will single you out for blessings. Divine favour will distinguish you among many people and you will stand out without being crushed. When the oil of favour is upon you, there will be open heavens for you irrespective of your circumstances.

CRUCIFIXION OF POVERTY

POWER TO SHINE

You need to understand how to draw upon the oil of favour. If you are able to provoke the oil of favour upon your head, your destiny will be beautified, the glory of God will shine in your life and you will move forward. The oil of favour is the key of promotion. When it comes upon you, you will outshine others. You will outrun those who have been running ahead of you. That is why the Bible says:

> *A good name is rather to be chosen than great riches, and loving favour rather than silver and gold.* Prov 22:1.

When you have divine favour, you do not need to bother about silver and gold. If you must have an uncommon success, it is important that you have divine favour. I remember the story of a very brilliant female doctor who applied to work abroad. Of all the doctors who applied at the said hospital she was the only black woman. The others were white.

They tried to pull her out of the contest but because she was divinely favoured, they could not. Even when she was given an examination, all the examiners gave her distinctions.

It got to a point that whenever she made a suggestion to the professors in that hospital and her suggestions were carried out, they would work perfectly. All the patients in the popular hospital would want to see her because whatever she prescribed as drugs for them was always backed up by heaven. This was because she had the oil of favour upon her head.

POWER TO STAND OUT

The oil of favour that is dropped on your head can be stolen. The ordination of favour from birth can be stolen just as virtues can be transferred. This is where warfare is necessary. You need to possess what has been lost. You have to possess what the enemy has stolen from you.

CRUCIFIXION OF POVERTY

If you want uncommon promotion you have to receive the oil of favour. You have to receive divine favour for you to receive breakthroughs and uncommon favour.

I remember a woman who went to an embassy to obtain a visa to travel out of the country. She was on the queue when a white man called her and asked what she came for. She said she came for a visa. The consular asked what she wanted to use the visa for. She told him that she wanted it to travel out to buy shoes she would sell here in Nigeria. The white man asked if she had enough money to start the business. The woman told him that she did not have but she would look for it as soon as she got the visa.

Normally with what she said, she was not supposed to be granted the visa but because she had the oil of favour upon her head, the white man collected her passport and told her to come back by 2 p.m. On getting there by 2 p.m. the visa was given to her.

The woman was the only person that was given a visa that day. That was divine favour at work.

You must receive divine favour to stand out and shine to the glory of God.

PRAYER POINTS

1. Strongman stealing my favour, die, in the name of Jesus.
2. Barriers to my favour, clear away, in the name of Jesus.
3. Oh God, arise and move me from labour to favour, in the name of Jesus.
4. Divine favour, locate my head, in the name of Jesus.
5. My season of favour, appear by fire, in the name of Jesus.
6. Every good thing that I have been looking for, begin to look for me, in the name of Jesus.
7. Every power that does not want my favour, die, in the name of Jesus.

OTHER PUBLICATIONS BY DR. D. K. OLUKOYA

1. A-Z of Complete Deliverance
2. Be Prepared
3. Bewitchment must die
4. Biblical Principles of Dream Interpretation
5. Born Great, But Tied Down
6. Breaking Bad Habits
7. Breakthrough Prayers For Business Professionals
8. Brokenness
9. Bringing Down The Power of God
10. Can God Trust You?
11. Command The Morning
12. Consecration Commitment & Loyalty
13. Contending For The Kingdom
14. Connecting to The God of Breakthroughs
15. Criminals In The House Of God
16. Dealing With Hidden Curses
17. Dealing With Local Satanic Technology
18. Dealing With Satanic Exchange
19. Dealing With The Evil Powers Of Your Father's House
20. Dealing With Tropical Demons
21. Dealing With Unprofitable Roots
22. Dealing With Witchcraft Barbers
23. Deliverance By Fire
24. Deliverance From Spirit Husband And Spirit Wife
25. Deliverance From The Limiting Powers
26. Deliverance of The Brain
27. Deliverance Of The Conscience
28. Deliverance Of The Head

OTHER PUBLICATIONS BY DR. D. K. OLUKOYA

29. Deliverance: God's Medicine Bottle
30. Destiny Clinic
31. Destroying Satanic Masks
32. Disgracing Soul Hunters
33. Divine Military Training
34. Divine Yellow Card
35. Dominion Prosperity
36. Drawers Of Power From The Heavenlies
37. Evil Appetite
38. Evil Umbrella
39. Facing Both Ways
40. Failure In The School Of Prayer
41. Fire For Life's Journey
42. For We Wrestle ...
43. Freedom Indeed
44. Holiness Unto The Lord
45. Holy Cry
46. Holy Fever
47. Hour Of Decision
48. How To Obtain Personal Deliverance
49. How To Pray When Surrounded By The Enemies
50. Idols Of The Heart
51. Is This What They Died For?
52. Let God Answer By Fire
53. Limiting God
54. Madness Of The Heart
55. Making Your Way Through The Traffic Jam of Life

OTHER PUBLICATIONS BY DR. D. K. OLUKOYA

56. Meat For Champions
57. Medicine For Winners
58. My Burden For The Church
59. Open Heavens Through Holy Disturbance
60. Overpowering Witchcraft
61. Paralysing The Riders And The Horse
62. Personal Spiritual Check-Up
63. Power Against Coffin Spirits
64. Power Against Destiny Quenchers
65. Power Against Dream Criminals
66. Power Against Local Wickedness
67. Power Against Marine Spirits
68. Power Against Spiritual Terrorists
69. Power Must Change Hands
70. Pray Your Way To Breakthroughs
71. Prayer Is The Battle
72. Prayer Rain
73. Prayer Strategies For Spinsters And Bachelors
74. Prayer To Kill Enchantment
75. Prayer To Make You Fulfil Your Divine Destiny
76. Prayer Warfare Against 70 Mad Spirits
77. Prayers For Open Heavens
78. Prayers To Arrest Satanic Frustration
79. Prayers To Destroy Diseases And Infirmities
80. Prayers To Move From Minimum To Maximum
81. Praying Against The Spirit Of The Valley
82. Praying To Destroy Satanic Roadblocks

OTHER PUBLICATIONS BY DR. D. K. OLUKOYA

83. Praying To Dismantle Witchcraft
84. Principles Of Prayer
85. Release From Destructive Covenants
86. Revoking Evil Decrees
87. Safeguarding Your Home
88. Satanic Diversion Of The Black Race
89. Silencing The Birds Of Darkness
90. Slaves Who Love Their Chains
91. Smite The Enemy And He Will Flee
92. Speaking Destruction Unto The Dark Rivers
93. Spiritual Education
94. Spiritual Growth And Maturity
95. Spiritual Warfare And The Home
96. Strategic Praying
97. Strategy Of Warfare Praying
98. Stop Them Before They Stop You
99. Students In The School Of Fear
100. Symptoms Of Witchcraft Attack
101. The Baptism of Fire
102. The Battle Against The Spirit Of Impossibility
103. The Dinning Table Of Darkness
104. The Enemy Has Done This
105. The Evil Cry Of Your Family Idol
106. The Fire Of Revival
107. The Great Deliverance
108. The Internal Stumbling Block
109. The Lord Is A Man Of War
110. The Mystery Of Mobile Curses
111. The Mystery Of The Mobile Temple
112. The Prayer Eagle

OTHER PUBLICATIONS BY DR. D. K. OLUKOYA

113. The Power of Aggressive Prayer Warriors
114. The Pursuit Of Success
115. The Seasons Of Life
116. The Secrets Of Greatness
117. The Serpentine Enemies
118. The Skeleton In Your Grandfather's Cupboard
119. The Slow Learners
120. The Snake In The Power House
121. The Spirit Of The Crab
122. The star hunters
123. The Star In Your Sky
124. The Terrible Agenda
125. The Tongue Trap
126. The Unconquerable Power
127. The Unlimited God
128. The Vagabond Spirit
129. The Way Of Divine Encounter
130. The Wealth Transfer Agenda
131. Tied Down In The Spirits
132. Too Hot To Handle
133. Turnaround Breakthrough
134. Unprofitable Foundations
135. Vacancy For Mad Prophets
136. Victory Over Satanic Dreams
137. Victory Over Your Greatest Enemies
138. Violent Prayers Against Stubborn Situations
139. War At The Edge Of Breakthroughs

OTHER PUBLICATIONS BY DR. D. K. OLUKOYA

140. Wasting The Wasters
141. Wealth Must Change Hands
142. What You Must Know About The House Fellowship
143. When God Is Silent
144. When the Battle is from Home
145. When The Deliverer Needs Deliverance
146. When Things Get Hard
147. When You Are Knocked Down
148. Where Is Your Faith
149. While Men Slept
150. Woman! Thou Art Loosed.
151. Your Battle And Your Strategy
152. Your Foundation And Destiny
153. Your Mouth And Your Deliverance

OTHER PUBLICATIONS BY DR. D. K. OLUKOYA

YORUBA PUBLICATIONS
1. ADURA AGBAYORI
2. ADURA TI NSI OKE NIDI
3. OJO ADURA

FRENCH PUBLICATIONS
1. PLUIE DE PRIERE
2. ESPIRIT DE VAGABONDAGE
3. EN FINIR AVEC LES FORCES MALEFIQUES DE LA MAISON DE TON PERE
4. QUE l'ENVOUTEMENT PERISSE
5. FRAPPEZ l'ADVERSAIRE ET IL FUIRA
6. COMMENT RECEVIR LA DELIVRANCE DU MARI ET FEMME DE NUIT
7. CPMMENT SE DELIVRER SOI-MEME
8. POVOIR CONTRE LES TERRORITES SPIRITUEL
9. PRIERE DE PERCEES POUR LES HOMMES D'AFFAIRES
10. PRIER JUSQU'A REMPORTER LA VICTOIRE
11. PRIERES VIOLENTES POUR HUMILIER LES PROBLEMES OPINIATRES
12. PRIERE POUR DETRUIRE LES MALADIES ET INFIRMITES
13. LE COMBAT SPIRITUEL ET LE FOYER
14. BILAN SPIRITUEL PERSONNEL
15. VICTOIRES SUR LES REVES SATANIQUES
16. PRIERES DE COMAT CONTRE 70 ESPIRITS DECHANINES
17. LA DEVIATION SATANIQUE DE LA RACE NOIRE
18. TON COMBAT ET TA STRATEGIE
19. VOTRE FONDEMENT ET VOTRE DESTIN
20. REVOQUER LES DECRETS MALEFIQUES
21. CANTIQUE DES CONTIQUES

OTHER PUBLICATIONS BY DR. D. K. OLUKOYA

22. LE MAUVAIS CRI DES IDOLES
23. QUAND LES CHOSES DEVIENNENT DIFFICILES
24. LES STRATEGIES DE PRIERES POUR LES CELIBATAIRES
25. SE LIBERER DES ALLIANCES MALEFIQUES
26. DEMANTELER LA SORCELLERIE
27. LA DELIVERANCE: LE FLACON DE MEDICAMENT DIEU
28. LA DELIVERANCE DE LA TETE
29. COMMANDER LE MATIN
30. NE GRAND MAIS LIE
31. POUVOIR CONTRE LES DEMOND TROPICAUX
32. LE PROGRAMME DE TRANFERT DE RICHESSE
33. LES ETUDIANTS A l'ECOLE DE LA PEUR
34. L'ETOILE DANS VOTRE CIEL
35. LES SAISONS DE LA VIE
36. FEMME TU ES LIBEREE

ANNUAL 70 DAYS PRAYER AND FASTING PUBLICATIONS

1. Prayers That Bring Miracles
2. Let God Answer By Fire
3. Prayers To Mount With Wings As Eagles
4. Prayers That Bring Explosive Increase
5. Prayers For Open Heavens
6. Prayers To Make You Fulfil Your Divine Destiny
7. Prayers That Make God To Answer And Fight By Fire.

OTHER PUBLICATIONS BY DR. D. K. OLUKOYA

8. Prayers That Bring Unchallengeable Victory And Breakthrough Rainfall Bombardments
9. Prayers That Bring Dominion Prosperity And Uncommon Success
10. Prayers That Bring Power And Overflowing Progress
11. Prayers That Bring Laughter And Enlargement Breakthroughs
12. Prayers That Bring Uncommon Favour And Breakthroughs
13. Prayers That Bring Unprecedented Greatness & Unmatchable Increase
14. Prayers That Bring Awesome Testimonies And Turn Around Breakthroughs.

BOOKS BY PASTOR (MRS) SHADE OLUKOYA

1. Power To Fulfil Your Destiny
2. Principles Of A Successful Marriage
3. The Call of God
4. The Daughters of Phillip
5. When Your Destiny is Under Attack
6. Violence Against Negative Voices
7. Woman of Wonder
8. I Decree An Uncommon Change

OTHER PUBLICATIONS BY DR. D. K. OLUKOYA

The Books, Tapes and CDs (Audio and Video)
All Obtainable At:

- Battle Cry Christian Ministries
  322, Herbert Macaulay Way, Sabo, Yaba, Lagos
  Phone: 01 8044415, 0803 304 4239

- MFM International Bookshop
  13, Olasimbo Street, Onike, Yaba, Lagos

- MFM Prayer City
  Km 12, Lagos/Ibadan Expressway

- 54, Akeju Street, off Shipeolu Street
  Palmgrove, Lagos

- All MFM Churches Nationwide

- All Leading Christian Bookstores

- Battle Cry Christian Ministries
  Abuja Zonal Office & Bookshop
  No 4, Nasarawa Street, Block A, Shop 4, Garki Old Market.
  Phone: 08135865868, 08159103039.

BOOK ORDER

Is there any book written by
Dr. D. K. Olukoya (General Overseer, MFM Ministries)
that you would like to have:

Have you seen his latest books?

To place an order for this End-Time Materials,

Call: 08161229775

Battle Cry Ministries... equipping the saints of God

God bless.